Manic Street Creature

Maimuna Memon

T0179854

methuen | drama

LONDON · NEW YORK · OXFORD · NEW DELHI · SYDNEY

METHUEN DRAMA
Bloomsbury Publishing Plc
50 Bedford Square, London, WC1B 3DP, UK
1385 Broadway, New York, NY 10018, USA
29 Earlsfort Terrace, Dublin 2, Ireland

BLOOMSBURY, METHUEN DRAMA and the Methuen
Drama logo are trademarks of Bloomsbury Publishing Plc

First published in Great Britain 2023

Cover image: Maimuna Memon, photographed
by Melanie Gail and edited by Charlotte Patmore

Bloomsbury Publishing Plc does not have any control over, or responsibility
for, any third-party websites referred to or in this book. All internet addresses
given in this book were correct at the time of going to press. The author and
publisher regret any inconvenience caused if addresses have changed or sites
have ceased to exist, but can accept no responsibility for any such changes.

All rights whatsoever in this play are strictly reserved and application
for performance etc. should be made before rehearsals to Knight Hall
Agency Ltd of Lower Ground Floor, 7 Mallow Street, London EC1Y 8RQ
(email: office@knighthallagency.com). No performance may be given unless
a licence has been obtained. No rights in incidental music or songs contained
in the Work are hereby granted and performance rights for any performance/
presentation whatsoever must be obtained from the respective copyright owners.

A catalogue record for this book is available from the British Library.

A catalog record for this book is available from the Library of Congress.

ISBN: PB: 978-1-3504-5748-5
ePDF: 978-1-3504-5749-2
eBook : 978-1-3504-5750-8

Series: Modern Plays

Typeset by Mark Heslington Ltd, Scarborough, North Yorkshire

To find out more about our authors and books visit
www.bloomsbury.com and sign up for our newsletters.

Manic Street Creature premiered at the Edinburgh Festival Fringe on 3 August 2022 at Paines Plough Roundabout at Summerhall. It was the recipient of the Fringe First Award, The Stage Award for Acting and The Mental Health Award.

CREATIVE

Music, Lyrics and Book	Maimuna Memon
Director	Kirsty Patrick Ward
Development Director	Bill Buckhurst
Sound Design	Sound Quiet Time
Lighting Design	Zoe Spurr
Producer	Joseph Dawson
Producer	Maimuna Memon
Creative Associate	Pia Ashcroft
Production Manager	Charlotte Ranson

CAST

RIA	Maimuna Memon
HEIDI	Rachel Barnes
RAZ	Yusuf Memon

Manic Street Creature transferred to Southwark Playhouse and had its London première on 19 October 2023.

CREATIVE

Music, Lyrics and Book	Maimuna Memon
Director	Kirsty Patrick Ward
Sound Design	Sound Quiet Time
Lighting Design	Jamie Platt
Set Design	Libby Watson
Producer	Southwark Playhouse
Producer	Maimuna Memon
Creative Associate	Pia Ashcroft
Stage Manager	Roni Neale
Movement Director	Ira Mandela Siobhan
Production Manager	Lee Elston

CAST

RIA	Maimuna Memon
HEIDI	Rachel Barnes
RAZ	Harley Johnston

Special thanks

To my mum Breda, my brothers Adil, Itrat and Yusuf and my Uncle Iqbal and Auntie Raine.

To Richard Gadd and Pia Ashcroft.

To Kirsty Patrick Ward, Rachel Barnes and Joseph Dawson.

To Sabine Chalmers, Michele Burns, The Genesis Foundation, Adam Kenwright, The National Theatre and Southwark Playhouse.

To Wildcard Theatre Company, Paines Plough and Sound Quiet Time.

To Bill Buckhurst, Marc Tritschler, Michelle Mangan, Tatty Hennessey, James Frewer and Harley Johnston

To Charlotte Knight, Samara Wash, David Lazenby and Jessica Francis.

To those who have listened to all my ramblings of ideas.

To those who have believed in my work.

To those who have pulled me out of the trenches.

Manic Street Creature

For my mum, who taught me what it means to be a strong woman.

Note on the text

Indented text indicates song lyrics, which are sung throughout.

Music begins. A swirling optimistic energy fills the space. In it are three musicians. **Ria**, **Heidi** *and* **Raz**. *They are facing each other.*

1. On My Way

Ria   We all ready guys?

ON MY WAY

Can I get a vocal from you both?

Heidi *and* **Raz** *harmonise.*

ON MY WAY

Ria *gives a thumbs up to the sound desk.*

Okay we're recording.

Light goes red.

ON MY WAY

Track 1. Take 1. 1, 2, 3, 4.

ON MY WAY, ON MY WAY
ON MY WAY, ON MY WAY
ON MY WAY, ON MY WAY
ON MY WAY, ON MY WAY
ON MY WAY, ON MY WAY
ON MY WAY, ON MY WAY
ON MY WAY, ON MY WAY OH
ON MY WAY, ON MY WAY OH

APRIL SUN
KNIGHTS ME AS A STRONG WOMAN
MIGHTY I HAVE BECOME
SUCCESS IS ON THE HORIZON

THE PATH IS CLEAR
DRIVING DOWN THE M40
CAR'S BURSTING TO THE SEAMS

BUT DON'T WORRY BOUT MY HEALTH AND
SAFETY NO

COZ I'M
ON MY WAY, ON MY WAY
ON MY WAY, ON MY WAY
ON MY WAY, ON MY WAY
ON MY WAY, ON MY WAY
ON MY WAY, ON MY WAY
ON MY WAY, ON MY WAY
ON MY WAY, ON MY WAY OH
ON MY WAY, ON MY WAY OH

Yes today I am driving from Lancashire to London
(Which in itself should be congratulated)
But more than that
Today is a fresh start

I'm staying in a flat near Camden Town station,
Lodging with two graduate nurses.
One of them's a friend of a friend
And had the room going for a decent price
£650 a month
Plus bills

Is she having a fucking laugh?!
I could rent a mansion in Blackburn for that.
But no, apparently 'that's a bargain for a bedroom in
Zone 2'
Which means absolutely nowt to me
But I guess I'll go along with it
And hope to eventually appreciate what she means.

MY ADOLESCENT EXISTENCE
IS A SHADOW IN THE DISTANCE
AND I'M NOT GUNNA MISS IT NO
LIQUIDATED MY OLD BUSINESS OH

ON MY WAY, ON MY WAY
ON MY WAY, ON MY WAY
ON MY WAY, ON MY WAY

ON MY WAY, ON MY WAY
ON MY WAY, ON MY WAY
ON MY WAY, ON MY WAY OH
ON MY WAY, OHHHHHHHH

Fuck! I missed the turning.
Why did I decide to *drive* to London?
Been chugging through this one-way system over
and over
Trying to avoid men on mopeds with serious anger issues.

Can't find the flat for at least an hour.
And when I finally find a parking space
It costs me about as much as my weekly food shop

COZ I'M
ON MY WAY, ON MY WAY
ON MY WAY, ON MY WAY
ON MY WAY, ON MY WAY OH
ON MY WAY, ON MY WAY OH

'Kin 'ell.
This is not Lancashire.
There are no good Samaritans now.
This is London. Camden Town. Zone 2.
And despite its gritty selfishness
I am happy to finally be here.

As I unload the last box into my box-like room,
I put my fitted bed sheet onto this inherited mattress.
And I realise that for the first time in so long
I am alone.

I wipe my sweaty moustache.
Unlatch my bedroom window
And breathe in the beautiful polluted fumes of North
London.

2. Set This House On Fire

Month two, London town.
I am HUSTLING.
I have gone into every pub, club, saloon
tavern, inn, lounge,
Café, restaurant, tearoom,
Hotel, pitstop, snack bar and public garden.
Offering my musical services.

'I WILL PLAY YOU A GIG FOR FREE
AND I *GUARANTEE* YOU WILL WANT ME BACK.'

To date payments for my services have included:
A fiver from an American man who felt sorry for me.

Tonight I am doing yet ANOTHER gig for zero cash.
At The Old Eagle
A rustic-looking Irish pub
Specialising in Thai cuisine
And seasoned with alcoholics
There are violins and mandolins and drums hanging off the
ceiling
And the smell of musty carpets
Reminds me of my local back home.

I think the only reason Juan the manager agreed to let me
play
Is because he was scared of me.

'I will play you a gig for free
And I guarantee you will want me back.'

So here I am. But I can't seem to find Juan?

Chords for 'Set This House On Fire' begin to play.

Instead, in his place
Is a blue-eyed lanky looking bloke
Draped behind the bar
In an oversized flannel shirt
Smoking a vape

And flirting with the pensioners
He looks at me with a blank expression
I can't tell if he's aware I'm meant to be playing tonight
Or if he even cares
Or if he can even . . . see me?
What a dickhead.

I want to shag him.

Indifference is the best turn on, am I right?
And there's one thing in my power
That I know will make him fall to his knees.

The lights bring focus to **Ria**. *She is in her element.*

> I COULD SET THIS HOUSE ON FIRE
> I COULD SET THIS HOUSE ON FIRE
> COZ I AM FILLED WITH THIS DESIRE

I've got his attention now.

> MY MIND IS LIKE A LIVE WIRE
> MY MIND IS LIKE A LIVE WIRE
> AND EVERY SECOND I CLIMB HIGHER
> EVERY SECOND I CLIMB . . .

At the end of the two 45-minute sets
I sit at the end of the bar
Sipping on tonic water
And chatting to the regulars about my Irish Heritage.
They're confused, naturally.
It's fucking brilliant.

1am
Me and flannel man haven't said a word to each other all
night.
He comes up to me now
And stuffs £80 in my hand.
I say:

What's this?

He says:

'You prefer to gig for a laugh then?'

No but. . .

'I'm the one cashing up tonight, so it's all good.'

You know, I think you're the first person to do something nice for me
In this dickhead city. Thank you.

'London can give life as quickly as it can take it.'

Well tonight provided a brief resuscitation . . .
Where you from?

'Glasgow. Yorkshire?'

Rookie error! Wrong side.
I'm Ria by the way.

'Daniel.'

The music for 'Set This House On Fire' begins again.

We walk back through the misty chill of the night.
Turn my key, unlock my front door
Lead Daniel upstairs
I never do this
He says:

'This place is cool. Must be expensive?'

Oh it's a total bargain for Zone 2.

Who the fuck have I turned into?!

Light goes red.

> SITTING ON MY BED
> AND YOU REACH OVER STROKE MY HEAD
> AND I GO
> OOO OOOO OOO
> OOO OOO
>
> NUDGING CLOSER SOFTLY YOU ASK
> CAN YOU SING FOR ME

AND I GO
OOO OOO OOO
OOOO

AND THEN YOU KISS ME OH
THIS NEVER HAPPENS OH
I STOP A MOMENT BUT
THEN I AM READY CUZ

I COULD SET THIS HOUSE ON FIRE
I COULD SET THIS HOUSE ON FIRE
COZ I AM FILLED WITH THIS DESIRE
I AM FILLED WITH THIS DESIRE
YOUR MIND IS LIKE A LIVE WIRE
YOUR MIND IS LIKE A LIVE WIRE
AND EVERY SECOND I CLIMB HIGHER
EVERY SECOND I CLIMB . . .

And then he sits at my keyboard and joins in.

You play?

'Yeah, bits and bobs.'

Bits and bobs my arse.
He's fucking good.
God, I am such a sucker for men who play music.
Regardless of whether it's the keys
Or the fucking French horn

LYING IN MY ROOM
YOU ASK ME QUESTIONS
I ASK YOU
YOU ANSWER OH OH
I ANSWER OH
THERE'S SOMETHING IN THE WAY
YOUR BRAIN'S ELECTRIC WHAT YOU SAY
IT MAKES ME OO OOO OOO
OOOOO

THIS NEVER HAPPENS HOW
I'M USUALLY GONE BY NOW

> BUT YOU EXCITE ME OO
> YOU MAKE ME WANT TO
>
> SET THIS HOUSE ON FIRE
> OH I COULD SET THIS HOUSE ON FIRE
> COZ I AM FILLED WITH THIS DESIRE
> I AM FILLED WITH THIS DESIRE
> YOUR MIND IS LIKE A LIVE WIRE
> YOUR MIND IS LIKE A LIVE WIRE
> AND EVERY SECOND WE CLIMB HIGHER
> EVERY SECOND WE CLIMB
> HIGHER
> EVERY SECOND WE CLIMB
> HIGHER
> EVERY SECOND WE CLIMB
> HIGHER
> EVERY SECOND WE CLIMB

A man who makes you orgasm
That's nice isn't it!
1, 2, 3, 4

> THERE IS SOMETHING IN THE WATER
> THERE'S A FEELING IN MY BONES
> WE ARE ONLY GETTING STRONGER
> I WANT TO SEE HOW FAR THIS GOES
> I AM TOSSING AND I'M TURNING
> I AM WAITING TILL THE MORN
> WHAT IS THIS ALL-CONSUMING YEARNING
> WHAT AM I FANTASISING FOR

One night turns into two.
Two weeks turn into four.
I am fiercely single.
I told myself London was about me and me only.
Fresh start.
But no one back home ever really understood what I was
trying to do.
And it's nice to spend time with someone who shares the
same dreams.

THERE IS SOMETHING IN THE WATER
THERE'S A FEELING IN MY BONES
WE ARE ONLY GETTING STRONGER
I WANT TO SEE HOW FAR THIS GOES
I AM TOSSING AND I'M TURNING
I AM WAITING TILL THE MORN
WHAT IS THIS ALL-CONSUMING YEARNING
WHAT AM I FANTASISING FOR . . .

At the tail end of the song we hear a phone ringing. Stage light goes blue. We hear a male voicemail: 'Hello this is Dr Ammar. Please leave your name and number and I'll get back to you as soon as possible. Many Thanks.' **Ria** *is in another place for a second.*

Heidi   Ria . . . happy with that take?

Ria   Yeah. Let's move on. Three and four and . . .

Straight into.

3. Insomnia

Mid-July
Roasting. BOILING.
All of a sudden sharing a bed with someone
Isn't so romantic
Especially when all fans are out of stock for a thirty-mile
radius.
The once charming energy of the main road my room faces
Now infuses my dreams with ambulance sirens.
It is small, hot and loud
And more often than not has a six-foot man
Adding a couple of extra degrees to the mix.

So . . . I guess Daniel is my boyfriend now?

He has been my introduction to London
Made my shitty keyboard sound sweet
Made music sound different in my ears
Made me want to transpose my thoughts
Into these notes and trills and chords
Made me feel like I kind of belong.
I've never felt like that before.

But I've also never slept so little.
And yes it's hot
And yes *he's* hot
But no that's not what disrupts the night.

He's been acting . . . strange.
Restless and twitchy.
Wired, on high voltage.
Eyes glowing in the darkness of the night . . .

Track 3.

Light goes red.

> WHEN I'M SLEEPING
> YOU AREN'T SLEEPING
> COZ THAT'S WHEN ALL YOUR DEMONS
> CREEP IN

AHH AHH AHH AHH
EYES ARE SPARKLING IN THE NIGHT
WIRED BRIGHT FLUORESCENT LIGHT
AHH AHH AHH

AND WHEN I'M SLEEPING YOU AREN'T
SLEEPING
I WAKE UP AND I RUB YOUR FEET AND
AHH AHH AHH AHH
I TRY TO FIND A PRESSURE POINT
I TRY TO COMFORT EVERY JOINT
AHH AHH AHH

INSOMNIA
STARING AT THE PALE MOONLIGHT
THROUGH THE BLINDS
WONDERING WHAT'S GOING ON IN YOUR
MIND
I'M TRYING TO KEEP MY
I'M TRYNA KEEP MY EYES WIDE
AS WE'RE LAYING HERE SIDE BY SIDE

And it's at that gentle juncture between night and day
Where the city softens for an hour or two,
That I start to really know him.
Here in my little room in Camden Town

AND WHEN YOU'RE SLEEPING
I'M NOT SLEEPING
I WATCH YOU MUMBLE IN YOUR DREAMS
AND
AHH AHHH
HOW YOU SCREAM INTO THE NIGHT
YOU TWITCH AND PANT AND SWEAT AND
SHOUT
I STROKE YOUR HEAD TILL YOU GET OUT
AHH AHH
YOU WAKE I HOLD YOU TIGHT

He says he gets these nightmares.
Wakes up shaking some nights. Pillow drenched in sweat.
And I sit there wishing I knew
The cause for his pain.

INSOMNIA
STARING AT THE PALE MOONLIGHT
THROUGH THE BLINDS
WONDERING WHAT'S GOING ON
IN YOUR MIND
I'M TRYING TO KEEP MY
I'M TRYNA KEEP MY EYES WIDE
AS WE'RE LAYING HERE SIDE BY SIDE

AND ANOTHER DAY OF HOPING
AND ANOTHER DAY OF WONDERING
IF WE'LL REST TONIGHT
BUT ANOTHER DAY OF KNOWING
IF WE CATCH THE GLOW OF MORNING
WE'LL STILL BE ALRIGHT
YOU'RE SO PEACEFUL IN THE LIGHT AND
I FIND IT QUITE SURPRISING
THAT I'M FEELING MORE THAN I
BARGAINED FOR
I CAN BARELY RECOGNISE
I CAN BARELY RECOGNISE
WHO I WAS BEFORE, WOAH

INSOMNIA
STARING AT THE SUN RISING
THROUGH THE BLINDS
WONDERING WHAT'S GOING ON
IN YOUR MIND
MY EYES ARE OPEN
MY EYES ARE OPEN WIDE
AS WE'RE LAYING HERE SIDE BY /

Sparse chords remain on guitar.

I LOVE YOU

YOLO do you know what I mean?

I LOVE YOU

I did say that pretty quietly . . .

I LOVE YOU

Maybe he didn't hear. So I say.

I love you.

And then he goes:

'Right.'

Oh dear.

Music pauses.

And I've never said that to anyone . . .
Never said that to anyone before in this context, I mean, so
. . . well I thought that was . . . quite brave . . . and, and . . .
you know, it would be quite nice to get your . . . thoughts.
On the situation.

Chords return.

'Ria, I . . . thank you . . .'

Mmm . . . not necessarily the response I was hoping for?

'Look, I think you are amazing. You are a much better
person than me . . .'

Oh please don't do the 'it's not you it's me thing . . .'

Beat kicks in.

'But it is. It is. Look, I've had some bad experiences in the
past and . . .'

And what?

'I've lost a lot of trust in . . . people and I just . . .'

Why you acting like this?

'Like what?'

Weird all of a sudden.

'I don't know what you're talking about . . .'

Oh come on Dan, just tell me what's going on.

'I just don't believe in love okay?'

Music stops.

But . . . you are my boyfriend?

'I'm not into those labels Ri.'

Oh fuck right off. Are you serious?

'You know what Ri, I don't need this fucking interrogation from you. I'm out.'

And with that, at 3am
Daniel grabs his phone and wallet
Storms down the stairs
And he's gone.

Ria *looks to* **Heidi**. **Ria** *moves to piano,* **Raz** *moves to harmonium.* **Ria** *nods to* **Heidi** *to move on. Straight into . . .*

4. Absent Father

And I don't hear from him.
I don't know where he's gone
What he's thinking.
Why he reacted like that.
I thought we had something . . .
But maybe that was too much,
Or I was too much to cope with
On top of whatever else he has been trying to cope with.

And now I have these *feelings*
These fucking *feelings* again.

I thought I had driven away from this.

Track 4.

Light goes red.

> ABSENT FATHER
> MAKES IT SO MUCH HARDER
> AND NOW I SEE NOW I SEE
> HE IS PART OF ME PART OF ME
> STARING OUT MY WINDOW
> CLUTCHING TO MY PHONE
> JUST LOOK AWAY LOOK AWAY
> HE WON'T CALL TODAY CALL TODAY
>
> MEN LIKE HIM GET AWAY WITH MURDER
> MEN LIKE HIM MAKE ME REACH OUT
> FURTHER
> MEN LIKE HIM I JUST WANT TO NURTURE
> ABSENT FATHER
> WON'T YOU TELL ME WHY
>
> AND NOW THE MAN I YEARN FOR
> SEEMS TO SHUT THE DOOR
> OH WAS IT ME WAS IT ME?
> OR MY HISTORY HISTORY?
> NOT DOING FEMINISM PROUD
> JUST WAITING AROUND

BUT THERE'S SOMETHING HE SOMETHING
HE'S
NOT TELLING ME TELLING ME

BUT MEN LIKE YOU GET AWAY WITH
MURDER
MEN LIKE YOU MAKE ME REACH OUT
FURTHER
MEN LIKE YOU I JUST WANT TO NURTURE
ABSENT LOVER
WON'T YOU TELL ME . . .

THIS IS VERY STRANGE
RECALLING WHO I WAS SOME YEARS AGO
A VERY TENDER AGE
WHEN A PARENT BROKE MY HEART
MY FATHER IS A CHILD
SO I COULD NEVER BE
AND FUNNILY YOUR SILENCE
TAKES IT BACK TO HIM AND ME

STILL MEN LIKE HIM GET AWAY WITH
MURDER
MEN LIKE HIM MAKE ME LOVE YOU
FURTHER
MEN LIKE THOSE WHO HAVE SO MUCH
HURT THERE
ABSENT FATHER
ABSENT LOVER
DON'T HURT ANOTHER
JUST TELL ME . . .

*The song is cut off by a dial tone. Light goes blue. We are in a
different time and space. We hear the voicemail again. 'Hello this is
Dr Ammar. Please leave your name and number and I'll get back to
you as soon as possible. Many Thanks.' 'Father Of Mine' motif plays.*

Hi Dad, it's me. Um . . .
Guess I just. Guess I just wanted to say I miss you.
Alright, um. Bye.

Light goes off.

5. Tell Me Your Secrets I Love You

Ria *begins underscore on electric guitar.* **Raz** *walks over to the acoustic guitar. The cello pedals.* **Ria** *turns on* **Raz**'s *musical entry.*

Fuck sake
Daniel's at my door.
Looking all fit and broken and stuff.

'Happy New Year.'

I stare back at him in cool silence
Trying to embody all of those female empowerment quotes
I've read on my Instagram feed.

'You look nice.'

I'm in my cat pyjamas.

And then he says:

'I love you. Too.'

I've waited so long for someone to say that to me
And actually mean it.
But no, I'm pissed off.

Thought you didn't believe in it?

'You changed my mind.'

Save me the cheese. Where the fuck have you been?

'I'm so sorry.'

You think you can just . . .
Turn up at my door after two months of silence?
This isn't *Love Actually* Dan.

'Ria look, I . . . I messed up. I am messed up. I'm just so scared of myself and my own brain.'

Dammit. Vulnerability is my weak spot.

'I love you Ria. And I'm sorry. Can you forgive me?'

Momentum kicks in.

Track 5.

He says he needs therapy, he'll get therapy. That he gets
depressed and obsessive and agitated about things. A history
of drugs and . . . and . . . he just didn't want to . . . tarnish
me with any of it and . . .

He was so naïve when he came to this city
And he wanted to make it so bad
That he trusted people too much and . . .

Light goes red.

       AND THEN HE TELLS ME EVERYTHING
       LIKE A CRUSHED-DOWN SPRING
       RELEASED AT THIS MOMENT

       AND THEN HE TELLS ME IT ALL
       LIKE A HEAVY RAINFALL
       IN THE FOREST

       I WANNA KNOW
       I WANNA KNOW YOU
       I WANNA KNOW IT ALL
       OOOOOOOOOO

       COZ YOU REMIND ME OF SOMEONE
       I USED TO KNOW
       CAN'T THINK WHO
       TELL ME YOUR SECRETS I LOVE YOU
       TELL ME YOUR SECRETS I LOVE YOU

I hear his words
His trembling voice
A man so deeply troubled
By the events of his past
And my chest burns for him
Emotions conjoined and
I now have this . . . purpose
I'm gunna help him
Make him better
Show him love he's never received

AND I WANNA KNOW
I WANNA CARE FOR YOU
I WANNA KNOW IT ALL
OOOOOOOOOO

COZ YOU REMIND ME OF SOMEONE
I USED TO KNOW
CAN'T THINK WHO
TELL ME YOUR SECRETS I LOVE YOU
TELL ME YOUR SECRETS I LOVE YOU
AND YOU MAKE ME FEEL LIKE I AM HOME
YET IT'S SO NEW
TELL ME YOUR SECRETS I LOVE YOU
TELL ME YOUR SECRETS I LOVE YOU

I ask him to join my band.
He is *insanely* talented.
We're at the studio as much as we can be.
I am writing songs relentlessly.

HOW CAN I HELP YOU?
HOW CAN I HELP YOU NOW?
OH I CAN HOLD YOU
TILL THE LIGHTS GO OUT
BLUE-EYED CHILD
BLUE-EYED CHILD
I PROMISE YOU
I'LL NEVER LET YOU DOWN

We move into a cute studio flat together in Dalston.
And by cute I mean
Just about big enough to not feel completely oppressive.
He wants matching bedside lamps
I think symmetry is the devil's work.

Pogues, 'Rainy Night in Soho' riff plays on the cello.

He introduces me to The Pogues.
Says they got him through the worst of times.

I stand on his feet
As we float around the house
To our newly chosen soundtrack.

> I'VE BEEN LOVING YOU A LONG TIME
> DOWN ALL THE YEARS DOWN ALL THE DAYS

His breath intensifies as he lets out a whimper.
Says that some music just gets him.
I never knew
That a man could be so open with his emotions like that.

He says, 'You can tell me anything you know?'

And I want to,
I really do
But . . .

> AND I CRIED FOR ALL YOUR TROUBLES
> SMILED AT YOUR FUNNY LITTLE WAYS

I introduce him to my mum . . .
First question to him of course: 'what do your parents do for a living?'

'Mum's a teacher, Dad's a scientist. What does your dad do again Ri?'

> HOW CAN I HELP YOU?
> HOW CAN I HELP YOU NOW?
> OH I CAN HOLD YOU
> TILL THE LIGHTS GO OUT
> THREE MONTHS GO
> FOUR MONTHS NOW
> I PROMISE YOU
> I'LL ALWAYS BE AROUND

Dan has an insatiable drive.
If he's not working at the bar
It's piano practice, or writing music,
Or anything
Anything to quieten the noise . . .

HOW CAN I HELP YOU?
HOW CAN I HELP YOU NOW?

And I love a strong work ethic,
But sharing a flat with someone
Can be tough
When that relentless motivation
Leads to denial of self-care

CLOSE YOUR EYES
CENTRALISE
TO THE HARMONIES
THAT ARE ALL AROUND AND . . .

I WANNA KNOW

There's a laugh I now can identify

I WANNA KNOW YOU

Maniacal, loud and incredibly high

I WANNA KNOW IT ALL

He wants to playfight
He catches my hair.

I WANNA KNOW IT ALL

Goes for a run
Gone for hours out there

OH I WANNA KNOW

Wants to buy a new shirt
But breaks down about which.

I WANNA KNOW YOU

Has a panic attack
'Bout a mark on the fridge

I WANNA KNOW IT ALL

Can't seem to get through
Was it something I said?

> KNOW YOU
> KNOW YOU
> KNOW YOU
> KNOW YOU
> KNOW YOU
> KNOW YOU
> KNOW YOU
> KNOW YOU

Music cuts out.

I find him hunched over the bed

Dan? Daniel, are you okay?

'I broke my favourite mug. I broke it.'

> OH YOU REMIND ME
> OF SOMEONE I USED TO KNOW
> OH I KNOW JUST WHO
> BUT I CAN'T HELP MYSELF
> I JUST LOVE YOU
> I CAN'T HELP MYSELF
> I JUST LOVE YOU

* * *

A bassy drone. Complete darkness during this pre-recorded call.

Phone   Hello, may I take your name please?

Ria   Ria Ammar.

Phone   And are you calling for yourself?

Ria   No. My partner.

Phone   And what's their name?

Ria   Daniel.

Phone   Surname?

Ria   Richardson.

Phone   NHS number please.

Ria   I don't have his NHS number. He's not in a fit state to tell me that right now.

Phone   Date of birth?

Ria   21st April 91.

Phone   Alright, and would you mind telling me how we can help your partner . . .?

Ria   He's just told me he's suicidal.

Phone   Okay, and is he on any medication?

Ria   No.

Phone   Okey dokey, any recreational drugs?

Ria   Not that I know of.

Phone   Okay, can we speak to him?

Ria   I've just said that he isn't in a fit state to /

Phone   If we could speak to him that would be best.

Pause.

Ria   Daniel. Dan, could you try to speak to the lady on the phone?

Daniel   I can't.

Ria   For me?

Beat.

Daniel   Hello?

Phone   Hello is this Daniel?

Daniel   Yes.

Phone   Can I have your NHS number please? /

Daniel   I don't . . .

Phone   Alright, date of birth then please?

Daniel   Urm. 21st April . . .1991.

Phone   Okey dokey, and can you confirm your last name please?

Daniel   Richardson.

Phone   Okay then, thank you Daniel. Now your partner says you are having suicidal thoughts.

Daniel   . . .

Phone   Hello?

Daniel   No. No. (*Whispering to* **Ria**.) I can't, I can't. Ria please take it.

Ria   You can hear he's clearly unwell. He's finding this very difficult.

Phone   Well he doesn't sound suicidal to me.

Beat.

Ria   He doesn't *sound* suicidal?

Phone   I can't do anything if he's not willing to cooperate.

Ria   This is fucking unbelievable.

Phone   We won't tolerate abusive behaviour on these phone calls.

Ria   Okay, well thanks for nothing.

* * *

Darkness . . . and then an explosion of light.

6. Why You Gotta Make Things So High?

The rhythm for the song starts. It's excitable. Almost manic.

No fucking wayyyyy

I have LOST my SHIT
Forget about getting signed to a record label
This is what dreams are made of.

A cat café!!

'Welcome to Claw-some Emporium! Happy one year anniversary Ri.'

Oh my god oh my god oh my god oh my gooodddd.

I've got half a dozen moggies surrounding me
A Turkish angora to my left
A Siamese to my right
Two Russian Blues staring at me across the room.
And an oat milk latte in my hand.
This is pure heaven.

Last night me and Dan had an amazing gig,
Followed by a catastrophic row.
Daniel started on the Peroni too early.
So thank god I was singing my tits off because
He was absolutely plastered by the second set.
Then he threw up in his backpack on the way home,
Told me I reminded him of his mother,
And fell asleep halfway through us having make-up sex
so . . .
Yeah. Eventful.

One year is a big milestone.
It feels like we have gone through what some couples won't
go through in five years, ten years,
Or ever.
So we *need* this.
We need the relaxing and healing power of cats.

'Aren't you a big fat fluffy fucking purring sweetheart?!'

How could I stay mad at this man?

Chords begin.

Owner   No picking up the cats please!

Daniel is stood at the other side of the café cuddling a
Russian Blue.

Owner   I said put Belinda down!

Belinda the Russian Blue seems apathetic.

Owner   Excuse me sir!

Daniel clearly has decided to ignore the owner of Claw-some
Emporium.

Owner   Sir!

Daniel has put Belinda onto his shoulder.
Belinda is looking confused yet stable.

Groove kicks in.

Daniel is now twirling around with Belinda on his shoulder.
Belinda is looking less anchored. Oh Jesus.

Owner   Sir! Sir!

I am imploring Daniel to stop.
But he can't hear me
His eyes are glittering with a frenetic mania.
And the owner is trying to remain calm yet assertive.
But Daniel is laughing now.
Eyes watering, unhinged. Almost possessed and . . .
I know that laugh all too well
It isn't a healthy one.
And I am taken right back to childhood
When my dad would lose his shit in a restaurant
And I would sit there helplessly
Covering my ears to drown out my mortification

Daniel trips.
Belinda flies off Daniel's shoulder.

She crash lands and scarpers behind a cactus-shaped cat scratcher.
And all the customers in the café fall silent.

Pause.

Owner   Please leave this café.

Fuck sake.

Light goes red.

WHY'D YOU GOTTA MAKE THINGS SO HIGH
WHY'D YOU WHY'D YOU DO IT?
I'D NEVER JUDGE YOU BUT
I SEE YOU BECOME WATERY EYED
AND YOUR MOUTH GOES DRY
AND I KNOW WHAT'S TO COME

OH WHY'D YOU GOTTA MAKE THINGS SO
HIGH?
WHY DON'T YOU HALT AND THEN REVIEW
IT
WELL YOUR EARS GO RED
YOU DON'T HEAR WHAT I SAID
I JUST CHEW MY GUM
YOU CAN'T SEE NO ONE

BUT YOUR HEAD BEAUTIFUL AND
BRILLIANT
YOU ARE TOTALLY MAGNIFICENT
YES YOU ARE
YOUR BRAIN FIREWORKS OF CHEMICALS
YOUR THOUGHTS PRECIOUS AND
ELECTRICAL
YES THEY ARE

SO WHY THE FUCK DID YOU DRINK LAST
NIGHT?
IT DOESN'T DO YOU ANY FAVOURS
A FEW HOURS THERE
YOU'RE WITHOUT A CARE

BUT THE MINUTE THAT YOUR LIVER'S HAD
ENOUGH

YOUR HEAD BEAUTIFUL AND BRILLIANT
YOU ARE TOTALLY MAGNIFICENT
YES YOU ARE
YOUR BRAIN FIREWORKS OF CHEMICALS
YOUR THOUGHTS PRECIOUS AND
ELECTRICAL
YES THEY ARE

YOUR MIND FULL OF MANY MEMORIES
THERE ARE SOME THAT BRING YOU TO
YOUR KNEES
IT'S NOT FAIR
YOU ARE UNLIKE ANYBODY ELSE
BUT YOU DO NOT KNOW HOW TO LOVE
YOURSELF

I DON'T WANT TO TELL YOU WHAT TO DO
I DON'T WANT TO STAY UP AT NIGHT FOR
YOU
I DON'T WANT TO ASK YOU WHEN AND
WHO
I JUST WANT YOU BETTER

As we sit in silence,
In our taxi home,
Dan says

'I feel like an alien in this city
Like I'm floating,
Disconnected to my body
Like I don't belong in this world.
I'm so sorry.
I wish my brain were simpler.'

And he cries.
And then he turns to me.

He says, 'I worry that I'm forever going to be defined by
my abuse.
By what he did to me.
That my brain has been permanently re-wired.
That I'll forever be a burden to you'

If only he could see how truly magnificent he is.

*Middle eight/father of mine motif. VM dial tone. Light goes blue.
'Hello this is Dr Ammar. Please leave your name and number and
I'll get back to you as soon as possible. Many thanks.'*

Ria   I could really use your advice at the moment, could
really use a male role model to tell me what the fuck to do in
this situation. Sometimes . . . I just . . . don't know how to
deal with things. Why can't you just pick up? You've never
fucking been there. Thank you for teaching me absolutely
nothing.

> I COULD SET THIS HOUSE ON FIRE
> I COULD SET THIS HOUSE ON FIRE
> WHAT IF I SET THIS HOUSE ON FIRE
> WHAT IF I SET THIS HOUSE ON FIRE
> MY MIND IS LIKE A LIVE WIRE
> MY MIND IS LIKE A LIVE WIRE
> DON'T WANT TO SET THIS HOUSE ON FIRE
> DON'T WANT TO . . .

* * *

Three knocks at the door with the drums. It catapults **Ria** *out of her
seat.*

I knock on the grand door
Of a freshly painted Victorian house in Highgate village,
North London.
Fuck me I should have become a psychiatrist.

A very short, very British man lets me in.
Shakes my hand. Directs me to a rather foreboding
And extremely red room.

I am no mental health specialist
But I already feel depressed in here.

Dr Collins   I'm Dr Collins.

Today Daniel has been having a session with a private
psychiatrist.

Dr Collins   Take a seat.

Whose hourly rate makes me want to shit myself.

Dr Collins   Now, Daniel has spoken to me at length about
his bipolar disorder . . .

Ria   Bipolar?

Dr Collins   Formerly known as manic depression. . .

We zoom in on **Ria**. *This hits her hard.*

Manic depression?
Manic depression. Oh.

Dr Collins   Now I've just asked Daniel to take a moment to
gather his thoughts.

Ria   Why?

Dr Collins   I was wondering if you could tell me a bit about
your experiences?

Ria   Mine?

Dr Collins   This must be very hard for you too?

Ria   I mean . . . I /

Dr Collins   You seem upset Ria.

Ria   I'm not.

Dr Collins   Are you worried Daniel's mental health could
jeopardise your relationship?

Bloody 'ell Dr Collins is firing on all cylinders!

Dr Collins   What do you do to look after your own mental health, Ria?

And somehow, what I expected to be Daniel's session
Has now turned into mine?

Dr Collins   Have *you* ever considered help?

Ria   I . . .

Ria *is about to say something. A moment. Then three knocks.*

And then Dan knocks at the door
Sits next to me.
He looks so pale. Head down. Ashamed.

What am I doing?
This is not about me.
This is about Dan.
Dan needs me.
So I hold onto him
We hold onto each other.

Dr Collins *watches on. Awkwardly British.*

Dr Collins   Ehem . . . now, although I don't agree that medication is the answer,
In the short term I think it could be beneficial for you Daniel.
Are you amenable to this?

7. The Middle

Track 7.

Black, into explosion of red light.

> ALL MY LIFE
> ALL I EVER WANTED WAS THE MIDDLE
> ALL MY LIFE
> QUIET, CALM.

It gets complicated from here
More complicated.
Real life isn't a straight road
It isn't even a winding path
It is a fucking obstacle course
That so often takes you right back to where you started

> SIMPLE'S UNCHARTERED WATER
> NEVER A MAGIC PILL
> NEVER SOMEONE TO TALK TO
> WHO SUDDENLY MAKES YOU WELL

And after months of different pills
Nausea
Headaches
Fatigue
Loss of appetite
And absolutely no sleep.
Daniel is finally prescribed olanzapine
And for the first time there is quiet, calm . . .

> THE MIDDLE

And virtually no side effects.
Except for one.
Detachment from me.

> SIMPLE'S UNCHARTERED WATER
> NEVER A MAGIC PILL
> NEVER SOMEONE TO TALK TO
> WHO SUDDENLY MAKES YOU WELL

NOTHING CAN EVER BE WRITTEN
THAT SUMMARISES YOUR HELL
BUT MAYBE A PRESCRIPTION
CAN HELP THE PAIN YOU FEEL

He falls asleep before me.
He's eating better
He's looking better.
Going out with his friends more.
Doesn't need advice now
He doesn't . . . need me.

THE MIDDLE
THE MIDDLE
ALL MY LIFE
ALL I EVER WANTED WAS
THE MIDDLE
THE MIDDLE
THE MIDDLE

It's . . . disconcerting.
It's suffocating.
Too quiet.
And who the fuck am I
To express this?
Maybe it's just in my head?
Maybe I was naïve.
Maybe this is what a normal relationship is like?
For so long I begged him to take action.
It's hard to know what's worse
Too much feeling or too little.

SIMPLE'S UNCHARTERED WATER
NEVER A MAGIC PILL
NEVER SOMEONE TO TALK TO
WHO SUDDENLY MAKES YOU WELL
NOTHING CAN EVER BE WRITTEN
THAT SUMMARISES YOUR HELL
BUT HERE IS A PRESCRIPTION
THAT HELPS THE PAIN YOU FEEL

And as I see him find the middle
I sink lower than I ever have before.
I know how to help people
I know how to make people feel good about themselves
I know how to be a shoulder to cry on
How to comfort, care for, console
That's what I'm good at. That's what I know.
And I'm jealous of that pill.
For taking my purpose away, and I just . . .

> I WANNA LOVE YOU
> I WANNA LOVE YOU
> I WANNA LOVE YOU
> I WANNA LOVE YOU
> LOVE YOU
> LOVE YOU

And without that purpose
Unwanted thoughts
Unhappy memories
Unfiltered emotions
Unwelcomingly appear and . . .

> SHALL WE PUT A RECORD ON
> SHALL WE SING OUR FAVOURITE SONG?
> NEVER SHUT ME OUT BEFORE
> NOW I FIND A BOLTED DOOR

Light goes blue. Father motif. 'Hello this is Dr Ammar. Please leave your name and number and I will get back to you as soon as possible. Many thanks.'

Ria Fuck you. Fuck you and all you ever said. I was stupid to think that you fucking ever cared.

> INSOMNIA
> STARING AT THE PALE MOONLIGHT
> THROUGH THE BLINDS
> WISHING THAT I COULD EXTINGUISH THIS
> NIGHT
> I'M TRYING TO SHUT MY EYES

Apathy is worse than
Hatred. Or disdain. Or even anger.
Because apathy is a void. A silent wasteland.
Nothingness.

Dan says he doesn't want to be in my band anymore.
That he needs to put himself first for a bit.
He's just not feeling music at the moment.
And he knows loads of people who can play for me anyway.

But then the real blow comes.

I've got a gig supporting one of my favourite bands.
At Bush Hall.
Singing songs I wrote about him. About us.
And I'm nervous. I haven't played a gig in a while
Because of everything that's been going on.
So this feels like a big thing. A big night.
And I didn't think I'd have to ask him,
I thought he'd just . . . be there.
But he doesn't show.

> INSOMNIA
> STARING AT THE PALE MOONLIGHT
> THROUGH THE BLINDS
> AS A NEVER ENDING RING IT RATTLES MY
> MIND
> I'M TRYING TO STOP BY BRAIN
> GOING A HUNDRED MILES

And as we lie in bed that night.
He just can't understand why I'm so hurt.

He says:
'I'm so busy at the moment
You know that.
If it meant that much to you, you should have specifically
asked,
And I would have made the space for it.'

Music stops.

Oh there's *never* any space for anyone else in your fucking
world, Dan.
I HATE you on these pills.

. . .

I shouldn't have said that I shouldn't have.
I don't know.
Fuck I shouldn't have said that.
We all say stuff we don't mean right? Stuff that isn't the
kindest.
FUCK why did I say that?

I guess I just . . .
Wanted him to be there for me.
Like I have been there for him.

And I don't want it to be transactional
I don't want to feel like this
Resentful of everything I've done,
Of the sleep I've lost, the stress I've felt.
Resentful of the support I have given,
The parts of myself I have surrendered.
But I do. I feel resentful.
Because I am getting nothing back.

Old Dan would have given me everything back.
But this Dan can't.
He's numb. Sedated by synthetic serotonin.
Instead he takes a double shift at the bar the next day.
And I feel more alone
Than I ever have before.

Maybe space is what we need?

* * *

I decide to go back up North for a little bit.
Spend some time with Mum.
A couple of weeks out of London.
No contact with Dan.
And I feel like that might be good for us.

Might help us to miss each other
Might help us to reconnect . . .

Twelve days go by.
And as usual,
The reality of home has left me writhing in an existential crisis

I get a text from Dan,
'Please come home.'

* * *

The cello plays an unnerving drone as **Ria** *picks up the electric guitar. Underscore begins.*

8. Manic Street Creature

It's an energy thing you know

As I get to our front door
I can feel the darkness
Seep under it
I walk into the flat
Silence.
There is a stink
From an unflushed shit Dan's left in the toilet
The heating is off. It's freezing
And Dan is sitting in a chair
In the middle of our room
Pale as a sheet. And shaking.

Dan?

He doesn't answer. So again I say.

Dan?

I go to shake him now.

'I couldn't do it.'

What couldn't you do?

'They were making me feel numb. I felt nothing.'

He's looking at the bin

He has crushed all of his pills
Into it.
FUCK.

How long have you not been taking them for?

Dan? DAN?

Light goes red.

> SHOULD I CALL THE DOCTOR?
> NO NO
> SHOULD I CALL YOUR MOTHER?

I DON'T KNOW
SO I'LL JUST SIT AND WONDER
OH OH
WHAT WOULD YOU DO IF I WASN'T HERE?
WHAT WOULD YOU DO IF I DISAPPEARED?

I MUST RESPECT YOUR BOUNDARIES
OH OH
TAKE YOU FOR YOUR WORD
WHEN YOU TELL ME NO
YOU'RE SMARTER THAN SO MANY
ALTHOUGH
YOU'RE NOT WHEN IT COMES TO A
HEALTHY MIND
YOU DON'T WANT TO STOP IN CASE YOU
GET LEFT BEHIND

SO YOU JUST RUN
SO YOU JUST RUN
WORKING ALL DAY
IGNORING THE SUN
MAKING EXCUSES
WHY YOU WON'T TALK TO NO ONE
MANIC STREET CREATURE
WITH YOUR TORMENTED TONGUE

CAN I CALL THE DOCTOR
WHY WHY
YOU MUSN'T SAY THAT WORD AGAIN
IT'S A WASTE OF TIME
THEY WOUDN'T UNDERSTAND EVEN IF
THEY TRIED
AND THE DRUGS AND THE WORDS AND THE
CBT
OH THEY DIDN'T WORK THE FIRST TIME
SO WHY TAKE RESPONSIBILITY?

RUN
SO YOU JUST RUN
WORKING ALL DAY

IGNORING THE SUN
YOU WON'T LET ME FINISH
YOU DECIDE WHEN WE'RE DONE
MANIC STREET CREATURE
IRRESPONSIBLE TONGUE
MANIC STREET CREATURE
WON'T YOU TALK TO SOMEONE?

I told you this story was complicated
And I know I said I wanted him to go on medication.
And then when he did I said I didn't like him on them.
Nothing is simple. There is no quick fix.
No magic pill.
But as someone I love more than anything in the world
The most important thing is that
He isn't suicidal.
And if that means he has to stay on those pills
That is what must happen. He is not safe without them.
So why? Why has he now decided to gamble with his life?

WHO WOULD HOLD THESE REINS IF NOT
ME?
WHAT IF I TORE ONE DAY
THEN WHO WOULD MEND ME?
WHO WOULD HOLD THESE REINS IF NOT
ME?
I'M ANGRY, I'M ANGRY.
WHO WOULD HOLD THESE REINS IF NOT
ME?
I'M ANGRY
WHAT IF I TORE ONE DAY, THEN WHO
WOULD MEND ME?
WHO WOULD HOLD THESE REINS
CAN I PICK YOU UP AGAIN?
I'M NOT SURE THAT I'M SANE

Middle eight underscore here.

Do you know how dangerous that is Dan? To just stop your
meds like that?

'You said you hated me on them.'

I'm so sorry Dan, I didn't mean it. I was upset.

'I took them for you. I never wanted to take them.'

For me? You took them for *me*? Why wouldn't you take them for YOU?! Why don't you value your own life? Why can't YOU take responsibility for your own mental health? Do you think I want you to be on pills, Dan? To be numb? Empathy-less? To have no inclination to touch me? Or have sex with me? Of course I wouldn't choose that! But there was no choice! There is no choice!

I STUMBLE

Feel like my brain's about to shatter.

I CRUMBLE

Does *my* well-being ever matter?

HE STUMBLES

He says I wish that this was over.

HE CRUMBLES

He says 'no don't come any closer'.

HE SEEMS POSSESSED
HE SAYS HE'S GOING TO FIX THIS MESS
HE WALKS TOWARDS ME AND HE CRIES
YOUR LIFE IS BETTER IF I DIE
HE SEEMS POSSESSED, DISTRESSED
HE SAYS HE'S GOING TO FIX THIS MESS
HE WALKS TOWARDS THE KITCHEN
DRAWER
SAYS I CAN'T DO THIS ANYMORE

HE SEEMS POSSESSED
HE SAYS I'M ALWAYS SO DEPRESSED
AND STRESSED I'M SUCH A MESS
HE TREMBLES AND HE CRIES

YOUR LIFE IS BETTER IF I DIE
HE SEEMS POSSESSED
HE SAYS HE'S GOING TO FIX THIS MESS
HE WALKS TOWARDS THE KITCHEN
DRAWER
SAYS I CAN'T DO THIS
I CAN'T DO THIS
I CAN'T DO THIS ANYMORE

A chaotic crescendo in the music. The lights go crazy. Slashes of light as **Ria** *lets rip.*

We hear her dial 999. The phone call is played out live.

Phone   Emergency services, which service would you like?

Ria   Ambulance.

Phone   Is the person breathing?

Ria   I think so. He's just hurt himself. It's really bad. Please help, please help.

The lights go crazy. **Ria** *loses her shit. And then a calm, a suspension, a focus. We have transcended time.*

Blue light. 'Hello this is Dr Ammar. Please leave your name and number and I'll get back to you as soon as possible. Many thanks.'

Ria   Dad, I can't keep calling you. I can't keep doing this to myself . . . I have tried, so hard. Kept myself awake. Made myself sick. Felt guilty, ashamed, blamed myself for your absence and your illness. I can't do it anymore. I am too tired. I'm going to leave you alone now. I hope you are okay. And I love you.

Light goes red.

SO HOW LONG WILL I RUN?
HOW LONG WILL I RUN?
WORKING ALL DAY?
IGNORING THE SUN
MAKING EXCUSES

WHY I WON'T TALK TO NO ONE
MANIC STREET CREATURE
IRRESPONSIBLE TONGUE

Light goes off.

* * *

Ria   Track 9.

9. Souls On The Precipice

There's this unspoken thing right?
I dunno. . .
I guess, this resistance to admitting
That someone else's trauma
Can be traumatising.

This is so fucking hard Dan.
Looking after you is fucking hard.
Exhausting. And painful. And depressing.
I feel like I've aged.

I worry about you every minute of every day
I wake up in the night sometimes and just watch you
To make sure you are still breathing.
I tie myself in knots thinking about you being on your own
Of you not eating, not sleeping.
If you don't text me back I convince myself you've . . .
Done something.

And then you *do* do something.
The worst happens
My biggest fear.
And . . .

And I realise that
That you aren't scared.
You aren't scared of the worst.
I'm scared. I'm so scared of losing you.

I have convinced myself that
I am responsible for you but
You never asked me to be.
And you survived before you met me.

I think I have this obsession with needing to fix things.
Coz if I can fix things, or make things better
Then I'm useful. I'm needed.
And if I *can't* fix things
Then maybe I dunno . . .

Maybe I'm just not worth the hassle. Not worth the love.
And love is all I have ever wanted.

My dad has manic depression too.
We uh . . . we don't speak anymore.
I don't know where he is.
I miss him.
Or at least the idea of him. Of having a dad.
And I'm really scared that he is going to die one day.
And I can't fix what's broken.

I ran away to this city to try and . . . forget.
So sitting here, with you, well it's uh . . .
Well it's funny isn't it? Who we are drawn to, who we love.

I love you.
So much. So deeply.
That I have used that as an excuse
To not love myself.

That's what I want to say.
But how can I say that to someone
Lying in a hospital bed
Bandaged and broken.
So I just hold his hand and say.

It'll be okay.
We'll be okay . . .

And then. He turns to me. Like he heard it all.

'Ria . . . We can't do this anymore, can we?'

'I'm a mess. And *you're* a mess. And we're totally co-dependent.
It's unhealthy. It's damaging.'

And I know he's right but . . .

All **Ria** *can do is sing.*

OH MY HEART
OH MY HEART

HOW LONG DOES IT TAKE FOR
A CRACKED WINDOW TO SHATTER?

HOW DO I START?
HOW DO I START AGAIN?
WHEN NOTHING ELSE IN THE WORLD
FEELS LIKE IT MATTERS?

STRANGE LITTLE THING YOU ARE
TRIED TO FIX AND FIX AND FIX AND FIX
AND FIX BUT
COULDN'T FIND THE RIGHT PARTS
YOUR CHAINS WERE RUSTING BRAKES
WERE CLICKING AND
OH, THIS WAS MY GREATEST FEAR
OH, THIS WAS MY GREATEST FEAR

I AM NOT A HEALER NO NO
I WASN'T MADE FOR THIS
I'VE GOT TOO MUCH FEELING OH OH
TOO MANY SOULS ON THE PRECIPICE
I AM NOT A HEALER NO NO
I CANNOT FIX MYSELF
I AM DONE WITH STEALING OH OH
THE PAIN OF SOMEONE ELSE

OH STRANGE LITTLE THING I AM
TRIED TO PUSH AND PUSH AND PUSH AND
PUSH AND PUSH AND
DO EVERYTHING I CAN
COZ TO EMBRACE THE DARKNESS BRINGS A
RUSH AND
OH, THIS WAS MY GREATEST FEAR
OH, THIS WAS MY GREATEST FEAR

I AM NOT A HEALER NO NO
I WASN'T BORN FOR THIS
I AM DONE WITH FEELING OH OH
TOO MANY SOULS ON THE PRECIPICE
I AM NOT A HEALER NO NO

CAN BARELY FIX MYSELF
I AM DONE WITH STEALING OH OH
THE PAIN OF SOMEONE ELSE
I AM DONE WITH STEALING OH OH
THE PAIN OF SOMEONE ELSE, BUT

WHAT IF I UNGROW
WHAT I UNGROW
SO I LEARN AND LEARN AND LEARN AGAIN
I WANT TO UNKNOW
I WANT TO UNKNOW
SO I CAN LEARN TO LOVE MYSELF AGAIN

WHAT IF I UNGROW
WHAT IF I UNGROW
SO I LEARN AND LEARN AND LEARN AGAIN
I WANT TO UNKNOW
I WANT TO UNKNOW
SO I CAN START TO SLOWLY GROW BACK UP
AND THEN

I'LL BE ON MY WAY
ON MY WAY ON MY WAY
I'LL BE ON MY WAY
ON MY WAY ON MY WAY

I WANT TO UNKNOW
I WANT TO UNKNOW
SO I CAN LEARN TO LOVE MYSELF AGAIN . . .

Ria *stops. She looks to* **Raz** *and* **Heidi**.

Raz Ria, did you get what you needed?

Ria Yeah.

Album is completed. The band share a moment. **Ria** *gives a thumbs up to the box. Red light goes off for the last time.*

Blackout.

End.

9 781350 457485